Disney's

Year Book 2004

FERN L. MAMBERG	*Executive Editor*
S. J. VICTORIA TUFFILL	*U.K. Editor*
ELIZABETH A. DEBELLA	*Designer*
KATHERINE M. SIEPIETOSKI	*Production Manager*

Articles designed by Northwoods Design Group
Stories and crafts illustrated by K. White Studio

PRINTED IN THE UNITED STATES OF AMERICA

ISBN: 0-7172-6877-2
ISSN: 0273-1274

Illustration Credits and Acknowledgments

6: American Philosophical Society; The Granger Collection; The Granger Collection; American Philosophical Society. 7: American Philosophical Society; American Philosophical Society; Artist, Gary Torrisi. 8: www. lewisandclarktrail.com; © Georgiana Harbeson/PicturesNow.com. 9: The Granger Collection. 10: © Frans Lanting/Minden Pictures. 11: © Zig Leszczynski/Animals Animals; © Rob Griffith/AP/Wide World Photos. 12: © Joe McDonald/Bruce Coleman Inc.; © Joe McDonald/DRK Photo. 13: © Dwight R. Kuhn; © Dwight R. Kuhn; © Art Wolfe. 28-29: © Phil Schermeister/National Geographic Image Collection. 30: © David M. Grossman/Photo Researchers, Inc.; © Phil Schermeister/National Geographic Image Collection. 31: © Phil Schermeister/National Geographic Image Collection. 32: © Massimo Borchi, Atlantide/Bruce Coleman Inc. 33: © Billy Hustace/Stone/Getty Images. 46: © Ron Gordon Garrison/Zoological Society of San Diego. 47: © Dennis Demello/Wildlife Conservation Society; © The San Francisco Zoological Society; © Dennis Demello/Wildlife Conservation Society. 48: Robert Harbison/© The Christian Science Monitor (www. csmonitor.com), all rights reserved. 49: © Frans Lanting/Minden Pictures. 50: © Edwin Giesbers. 51: © Fritz Polking/Bruce Coleman Inc.; © Nick Garbutt/naturpl.com; © Dennis MacDonald/PhotoEdit; © Michael Fogden/Bruce Coleman Inc./PictureQuest; © Michael Fogden/DRK Photo. 52: © Phil A. Dotson/ Photo Researchers, Inc.; © Bruce Coleman Inc./PictureQuest. 53: © Ulrike Welsch/PhotoEdit; © Janice Sheldon/Photo 20-20/PictureQuest. 68: Superstock. 69: © Giorgio Gualco/Bruce Coleman Inc.; Superstock; © Coco McCoy/Rainbow/PictureQuest. 70: © Melloan/PhotoEdit; © Adam Woolfitt/Woodfin Camp & Associates. 71: Don Cole/UCLA Fowler Museum of Cultural History. 72: © Gerard Lacz/Animals Animals; © F. J. Hiersche/Okapia/Photo Researchers, Inc. 73: © Sid Bahrt/Photo Researchers, Inc.; © Tui De Roy/Bruce Coleman Inc.; © C. K. Lorenz/Photo Researchers, Inc. 86: © Adam Butler/AP/Wide World Photos. 87: © Steve Holland/AP/Wide World Photos; © Adam Butler/AP/Wide World Photos. 88: © Paul Harris/Online USA/Getty Images; © Steve Holland/ AP/Wide World Photos; © Mark Lennihan/ AP/Wide World Photos. 89: © Amy E. Conn/AP/Wide World Photos; © Getty Images. 90: © Dave B. Fleetham/Tom Stack & Associates; © Fred Bavendam. 91: © Denise Tackett/Tom Stack & Associates; © Larry Lipsky/DRK Photo. 92: © Juergen & Christine Sohns/Animals Animals; © Stephen J. Krasemann/ DRK Photo. 93: © G. Hinde, ABPL/Animals Animals; © K&K Ammann/Bruce Coleman Inc. 94: © Fred Bavendam/Minden Pictures; © Fred Bavendam. 95: © Michael Fogden/DRK Photo.

Disney's

Year Book 2004

SCHOLASTIC INC.
New York • Toronto • London • Auckland • Sydney •
Mexico City • New Delhi • Hong Kong • Buenos Aires

Contents

BLAST FROM THE PAST

Meriwether Lewis (left) and William Clark (right) explored the West in 1804-06. Their journals, which included drawings, described everything they found.

Lewis & Clark:

A Great Adventure

In 1804, no one was sure what lay between the Mississippi River and the Pacific Ocean. So a great expedition was mounted to explore the western United States. The explorers knew only that the voyage of discovery would be long and hard—and dangerous!

Meriwether Lewis and William Clark led the expedition. Thanks to them, the wonders of the West were revealed at last. This year marks the 200th anniversary of their trip. It was a great adventure!

Lewis and Clark found lots of new plants on their journey. These two plants were named for them—*Lewisii* (left) and *Clarkia* (right).

The trip was President Thomas Jefferson's idea. Jefferson hoped Lewis and Clark would find a way to reach the Pacific Ocean by boat. He also wanted them to discover everything they could about the West.

Lewis and Clark left St. Louis, Missouri, on May 14, 1804. With them were about 30 soldiers. They headed up the Missouri River in boats. Their long journey had begun.

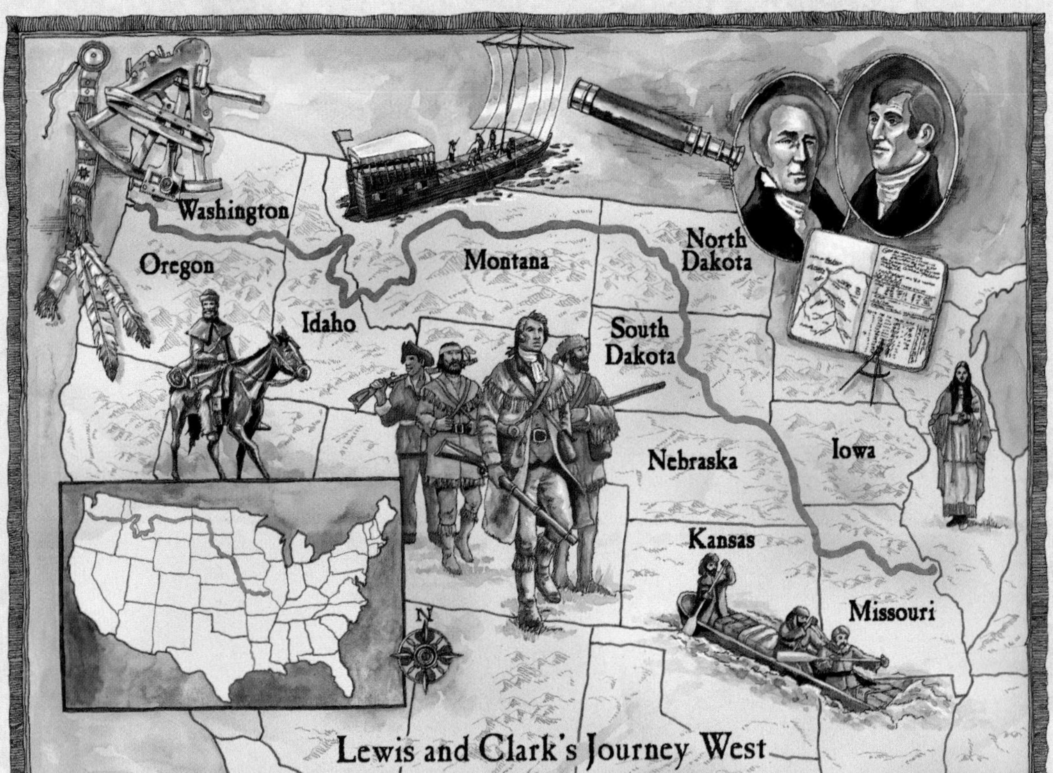

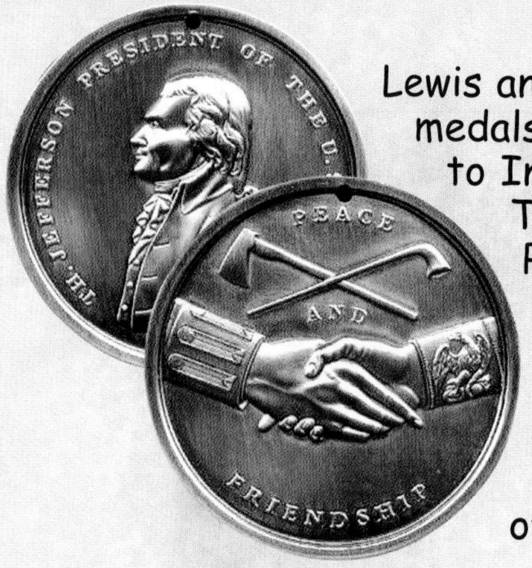

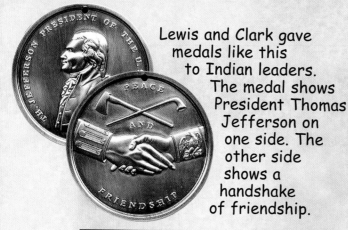

Lewis and Clark gave medals like this to Indian leaders. The medal shows President Thomas Jefferson on one side. The other side shows a handshake of friendship.

The explorers paddled upriver for many miles. They saw all kinds of animals—prairie dogs . . . and bison . . . and grizzly bears! And they met many American Indians, who often helped them.

Lewis and Clark spent the winter near an Indian village in what is today North Dakota. In the spring, they headed upriver again. Ahead lay miles and miles of flat plains. And beyond the plains were the tall Rocky Mountains.

To cross the mountains, Lewis and Clark had to leave their boats. They travelled on foot, with horses carrying their equipment. They nearly ran out of food. But they made it!

Sacagawea

Sacagawea (sak-a-ja-WE-a) was the only woman on the journey. She was the wife of a trapper who was hired as a guide. She was a remarkable person!

Sacagawea was a Shoshoni Indian. She spoke several Indian languages. She helped the explorers talk and trade with the Indians they met. And she helped them get horses for the trip over the Rocky Mountains.

Sacagawea carried her newborn son with her. Seeing a woman and a baby, the Indians knew that the travellers were peaceful, and they let them pass.

Let's go out west for an adventure!

Pictures from an 1811 book show events along the trail. A bear chases a hunter up a tree. The explorers build huts. Lewis and Clark meet with Indians. A canoe tips over.

Beyond the mountains, Lewis and Clark stopped to make new boats. Then they headed down a series of rivers. In November 1805 they finally reached the Pacific Ocean!

The explorers spent the winter on the Pacific Coast, in present-day Oregon. Then they made the long trip home, back over the mountains and across the plains. They reached St. Louis in September 1806. They were greeted as heroes, and they told everyone about the wonders they had seen. Soon many other explorers and settlers headed west.

ANIMAL MAGICIANS

The chameleon is famous because it can change colour. But it is amazing in other ways, too!

Chameleons are animal magicians. They can change colour! And that's not the only trick these animals can do.

Chameleons are lizards. There are about 90 different kinds. Some are longer than your arm. Others are smaller than your thumb. They make their homes in warm places, mostly in Africa and Asia.

Most chameleons are green or brown. Some may have yellow, blue, red, and black on their bodies, too. But their colours and patterns can change in the blink of an eye!

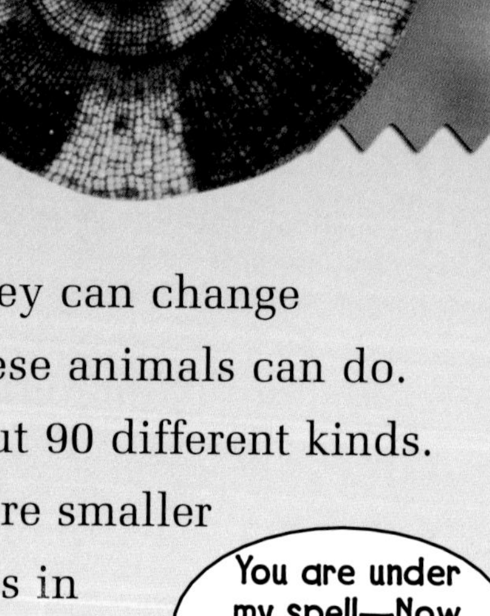

You are under my spell—Now turn into a chameleon!

CHECK OUT THIS ACT!

Like other lizards, chameleons hatch from eggs.

The chameleon's trick isn't really magic. Sometimes a change in temperature or light causes the colour change. Warmth and sunlight darken the lizard's colours. Coolness and shade make the colours lighter.

Moods can also make these animals change their hues. When a chameleon is scared, its colours are dull. When it's angry, its colours are dark.

Some chameleons are only a couple of inches long. And some are a couple of feet long!

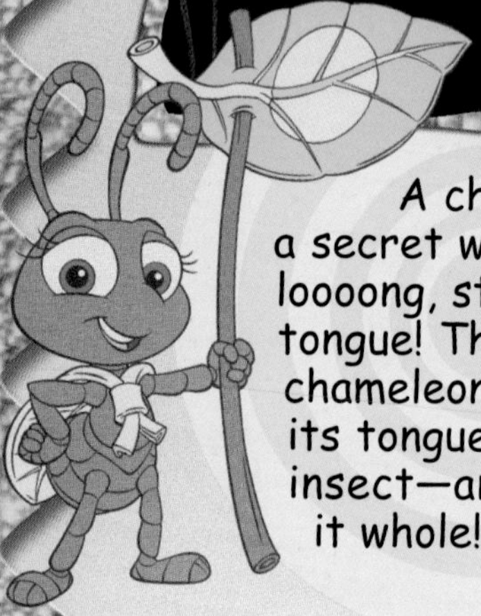

A chameleon has a secret weapon: its looooong, sticky-tipped tongue! The hungry chameleon shoots out its tongue to catch an insect—and swallows it whole!

Males may change colour to attract mates. Rival males even have colour wars. They face off and try to scare each other, turning bright colours!

How does a chameleon perform this trick? Its skin has layers of colour cells. The cells in each layer have different pigments—chemicals that create colour. Light, warmth, and moods affect the cells, so the pigments shift.

Here's another chameleon trick. This lizard can look in two different directions at once. One eye can look forwards, while the other eye looks back.

Chameleons are amazing in still other ways. A chameleon's tongue may be as long as its body!

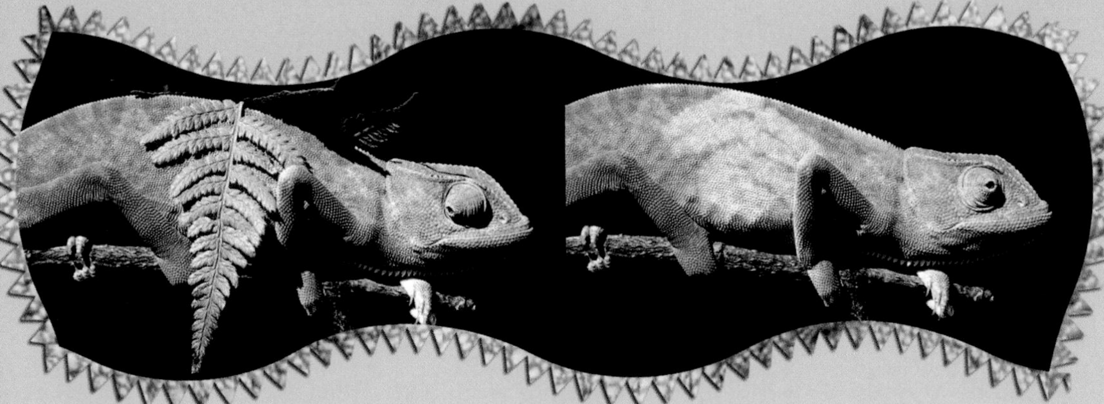

Shade makes a chameleon go pale. When a fern leaf is taken off a chameleon's back (above), a pale "print" is left behind.

Most chameleons live in trees. They use their grasping claws to climb. Their long tails help, too. A chameleon can grip with its tail. Most of the time, the tail stays coiled up. But when the chameleon needs to hang on extra tight, it wraps its tail around a branch.

This animal magician knows LOTS of tricks!

Did You Know?

A chameleon's bulging eyes are covered by scaly lids. The eyes can move in two different directions at the same time!

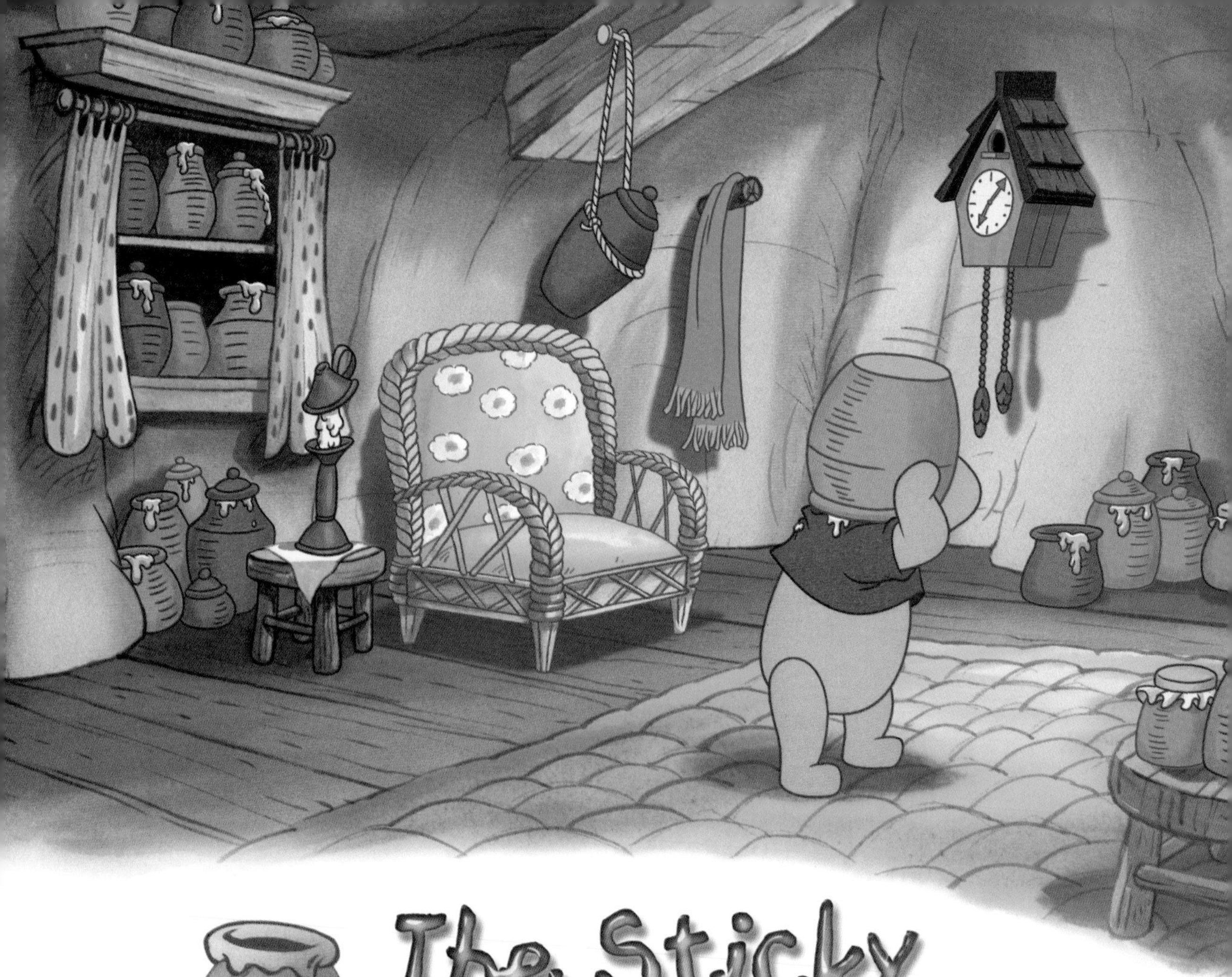

The Sticky Honey Pot

“Oh, fluff and stuff!” said Pooh in an echo-ey sort of voice. You see, Pooh had got his head stuck in a pot of honey while trying to lick the very last bit of the sticky sweet stuff from the bottom of the pot. Now Pooh’s head had been stuck in honey pots before, and it would remain there until he managed to twist and wiggle himself free . . . or until someone came along to pull the pot off for him.

Right now, however, Pooh was really in a lot of trouble. His head was wedged quite tightly, and there was no one around. So he decided to look for help. Unfortunately, having a pot on one's head makes looking for others somewhat difficult.

Bump! Thump!

"Oh, double bother!" Pooh said inside the pot. The bump had been made by his bumping into something in his house. The thump had been the sound of his backside landing on the floor immediately after the bump.

How was Pooh going to find someone to help him? Then he had an idea. This made Pooh rather proud, as bears of very little brain don't often have ideas.

"I shall find my way outside, where someone will find me!" he decided.

Feeling very pleased with himself, Pooh managed to find a way (with a few more bumps and thumps) of moving across the room to his open door.

"Lovely," Pooh said to himself (only it sounded more like "lumply" from inside the honey pot). "Now I shall simply wait for someone to rescue me."

So he did.

Pooh waited and waited. And waited. He tried humming to himself but got confused by the echoes, so he stopped. Then he tried tapping his foot, but that didn't seem to be all that interesting. At last, Pooh fell asleep.

After a bit, Pooh's good friend Piglet came for a visit. When Piglet saw his friend sitting on a tree stump outside his door with a honey pot on his head and making a strange noise, he was puzzled.

"Pooh?" asked Piglet tentatively.

"Mmmmmmmm-pffff. Mmmmmmm-pffffff," said Pooh.

"Oh, did I interrupt your lunch?" asked Piglet. "Perhaps I should come back later."

"Um-hmmmm." Pooh was snoring, but Piglet thought Pooh had said "Uh-huh," as in, "Yes, please do return

later." So Piglet left without Pooh ever even knowing he had been there.

Soon after, Tigger arrived at Pooh's house.

"Hiya, Pooh Bear!" Tigger bounced on top of Pooh.

"Oof! Oof!" said Pooh. To Tigger, it sounded as if Pooh had said "Hoo-hoo!"

"That's right, Pooh!" cried Tigger. "I say that, too. Only sometimes I add an extra 'HOO!' to make it extra-specially tiggery. Hoo-hoo-HOO!"

Pooh didn't hear a thing Tigger was saying. He was simply trying to catch his breath after being bounced.

"Well," said Tigger. "I got some more bouncin' ta do. See ya later, Pooh Bear. Hoo-hoo-HOO!"

Tigger bounced Pooh one last time before he left, leading Pooh to say once again, “Oof!” This delighted Tigger, as he believed Pooh was talking to him.

Soon evening fell, and Pooh stumbled inside his house and closed the door. He sat down in his comfy chair, wondering if someone might still come to

rescue him. He was hoping that the someone might come sooner rather than later. His rumbly tummy was telling him it was way past both tea and supper time.

At last there came a loud rapping at Pooh's door, which, of course, Pooh couldn't hear at all.

Christopher Robin popped his head inside Pooh's front door and found his favourite bear sitting quietly in his comfy chair with a honey pot wedged tightly over his head.

"Oh, Pooh, you silly old bear!" said Christopher Robin playfully. "I've been looking everywhere for you. I haven't seen you all day, and I thought—"

Christopher Robin suddenly stopped talking. He realized that Pooh could probably not hear a word he was saying. So he went over to Pooh and tapped very gently on the honey pot.

Pooh sat up straight and shouted, “Come on in!” He thought someone was knocking at his door. All Christopher Robin heard was, “Kooo-eeee!”

Christopher Robin had seen Pooh stuck in this type of situation before. He began to twist and turn the pot very gently to try to get it off Pooh’s head. But no matter which way he twisted, turned, and pulled at the honey pot, it simply would not budge.

Then he had an idea. He went over to Pooh's kitchen sink and got a cloth and dipped it into some warm, soapy water. Carefully he wiped away the gooey honey that was sticking all around Pooh's head and neck.

After a while, Christopher Robin gave one last yank on the honey pot.

Pop!

Off came the pot, and out popped Pooh's head.

"Oh, hello, Christopher Robin!" Pooh said excitedly. "I was hoping you might turn up. You see, I have this pot stuck on my head, and I thought you might be able to help me get it off."

"Silly old bear!" said Christopher Robin. "Look! It's already off your head! That's why you can see me and hear me!"

"Oh," said Pooh. "Well, in that case, thank you very much for your help!"

So, feeling rather generous and grateful, Pooh asked Christopher Robin to stay for supper with him. Christopher Robin gladly accepted, and the two good friends had a wonderful evening.

And when Pooh began to look at the bottom of his honey pot to finish off the very last smackerel of his delicious supper, Christopher Robin made sure that the bear used his paw instead of his head to get it!

TRY THIS!

Fantasy Flowers

These pretty fantasy flowers are made from colourful tissue paper. They are fun to make. You can keep them or give them to a special person.

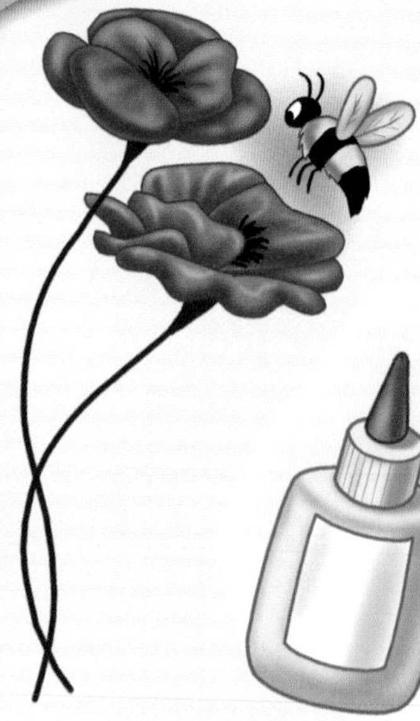

What You Need

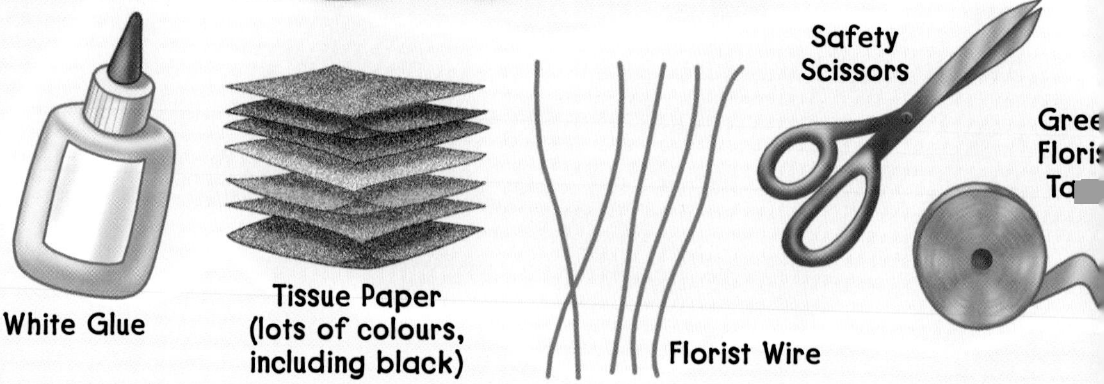

What You Do

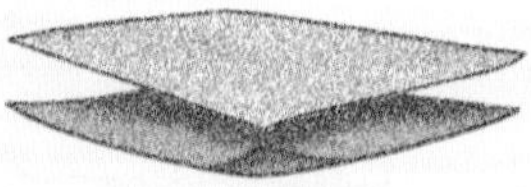

1. Crumple up a small piece of green tissue paper. Glue it onto one end of a piece of wire. This will be the centre of the flower.

2. Take a small piece of black tissue paper. Cut a fringe along one edge. Glue the fringed paper around the centre of the flower. Fluff the fringe out a bit.

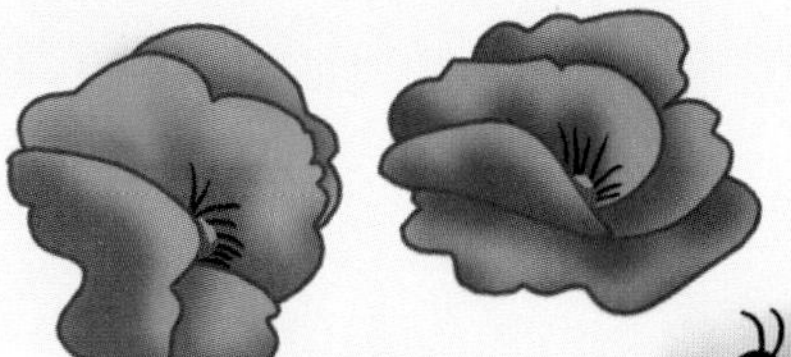

3. Cut out three or four round circles of colourful tissue paper. Scallop the edges of each one. These are the petals. Poke a small hole in the centre of each petal.

4. Thread each petal onto the wire, from the bottom up. Push it up to the base of the fringed paper.

5. Wrap the green florist tape around the wire. Start at the top of the wire, below the petals.

Make lots of coloured flowers. Put them in a vase and you'll have a rainbow bouquet!

Let's CELEBRATE

Chines

The Dragon Dance is an exciting part of the Chinese New Year celebration.

Do you know what year it is? Yes, it's 2004. But in the Chinese calendar, it's the Year of the Monkey!

The Chinese calendar is very old. No one knows how it began. As in the Western calendar, each year has twelve months. But the Chinese name each year for one of twelve animals. And the names are repeated every twelve years.

The Chinese celebrate the New Year when the first new moon of the year appears. The date changes from year to year.

New Year

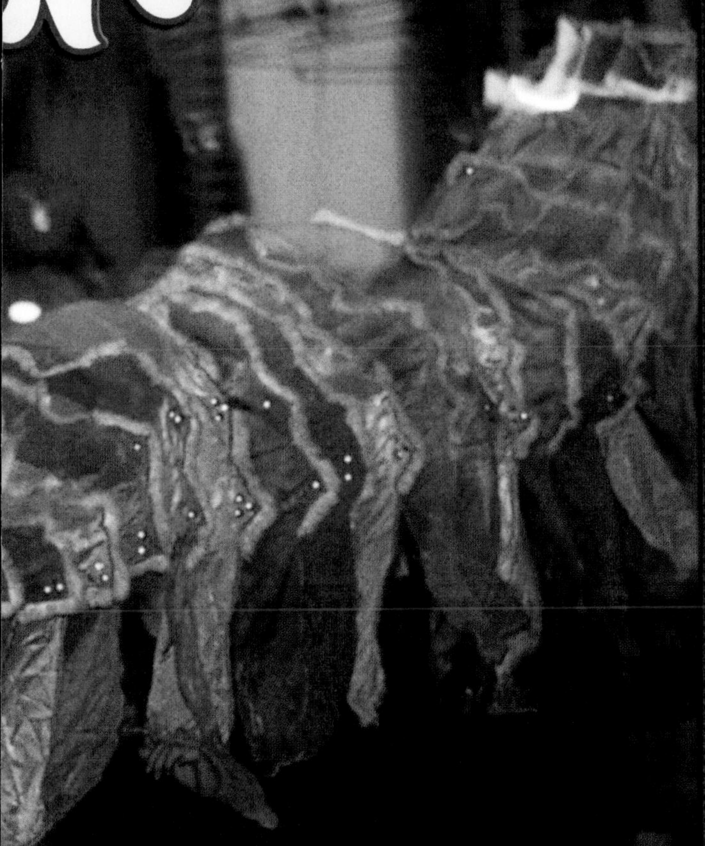

Sometimes the Chinese New Year falls in late January. Sometimes it's in February. But it's always a time for lots of fun. People spend weeks getting ready for this holiday. They buy new clothes. And they clean their houses from top to bottom.

Kitchen God's Day

A picture of the Kitchen God hangs in many Chinese homes. All year, this god is said to watch the family. Then, at the end of the year, the Kitchen God returns to heaven. There he reports everything the family has done to the Jade Emperor, the ruler of heaven.

Kitchen God's Day comes a week before the Chinese New Year. On this day, the god's picture is taken down. Firecrackers are set off to send the god on his way to heaven. But before he goes, the family may brush his lips with honey—so he will have only sweet things to say about the family!

The Kitchen God's place stands empty until New Year's Eve. Then the family hangs up a new picture to welcome him back.

Chinese Zodiac

Each year in the Chinese calendar is named for an animal. Tradition says that a person's animal sign shows his or her character. Find your animal sign by looking for your birth year below. Does your character match your sign?

Then the New Year holiday begins—with a bang! On New Year's Eve firecrackers go off. The loud noises are meant to scare away bad spirits.

The holiday fun goes on for days. Families get together. They give gifts and share delicious feasts. Food is laid out to honour the family ancestors. There are lots of special New Year's foods, such as sweet rice pudding.

Chinese children are given "good luck" money for the New Year. The money is put in red envelopes. Red is thought to be the luckiest colour. The Chinese writing on the envelopes means good wishes.

Monkey
(2004, 1992)

You are clever and charming. You love adventure. And sometimes you get in trouble!

Sheep
(2003, 1991)

You are gentle and a little baa-shful. You are also creative and a good friend.

Horse
(2002, 1990)

You are cheerful, helpful, loyal, and clever. But sometimes you talk too much!

Many of the foods carry meanings. For example, long noodles stand for long life.

Lots of traditions are linked to the Chinese New Year. Most are meant to bring good luck in the year ahead. Knives are put away. They might "cut" someone's luck. And people don't wash their hair on New Year's Day. That might wash away good luck!

Did You Know?

Sweet foods that are eaten on New Year's Day are said to bring a sweet year.

I'll put away my sword on New Year's Day so I won't "cut" my luck!

Snake
(2001)

You are a quiet one, but you are ssssmart. You are also artistic and full of energy.

Dragon
(2000)

You are lucky, healthy, and brave. But your temper can be fiery!

Rabbit
(1999)

You are talented, and you want to get ahead. If there's something to do, you hop to it!

The Lion Dance

The Lion Dance is a high point of any New Year celebration. Two dancers bring the lion to life. One is at the front end, working the head. The other is at the back. Together, they make the lion leap and dance through the streets. Three musicians go along. They play a drum, cymbals, and a gong. A well-performed Lion Dance is said to bring good luck.

Dragons are said to bring good luck, too. People line the streets to watch the Dragon Dance. In this colourful parade, dancers carry a long paper dragon through the streets. Another New Year favourite is the Lion Dance.

For everyone, the New Year is a time for fresh starts. Old debts are paid. Even old arguments are forgotten when the New Year begins. Tradition says that enemies must forgive and forget. Everyone must be friends—at least for the first week of the year!

Tiger (1998)

You are friendly and thoughtful. You also have courage—and can roar!

Ox (1997)

You are a calm and patient leader. You are strong and always pull your weight!

Rat (1996)

You are charming and creative. But sometimes you have a quick temper!

The New Year is the most important holiday in China. And it's celebrated in countries all over the world. Wherever Chinese people have settled, they enjoy this special time. In the United Kingdom, there are big parades in the Chinatowns of London and other cities. People gather to celebrate. They shout "Gung Hay Fat Choy"—Happy New Year!

The Lantern Festival

The Lantern Festival marks the end of the Chinese New Year season. Children carry beautiful coloured lanterns through the streets. More lanterns hang on homes and temples. There are fireworks, dancing, and plenty of other fun.

Dragons bring good luck!

Where's the Year of the Cricket?!

Pig
(1995)

You are brave and strong. You are kind and loving, too. You are never a hog!

Dog
(1994)

You are loyal, funny, and honest. You are the leader of the pack!

Rooster
(1993)

You are confident. You like to crow! But your friends can count on you.

The Bird-Sitters

"And this, Simba, is precisely why I ask you to stay close to me!" Zazu said. "Just look around you!"

Simba hung his head, then made himself look around. He and Nala were surrounded by a herd of elephants—angry elephants that had been stampeding just moments ago. Zazu flapped his wings, then perched on the elephant leader's head, just between his long, floppy ears.

"I didn't mean to make them run, Zazu," Simba said. "Honest. Nala and I were playing tag, and I think they just misunderstood."

Zazu flew in front of Simba to look him in the eye. "Yelling, 'Run for your life!' had nothing to do with it?"

"We were just joking, Zazu," said Nala.

"We'll be more careful," Simba promised. "Um, you won't tell my dad will you, Zazu?"

"Hmm," Zazu ruffled his feathers. "Well, I suppose I could do you a favour if . . ."

"If what?" said Simba.

"Well," Zazu said, "it just so happens that my young niece Zinga will be visiting tomorrow while I have important business with the king. If you'll apologize to the elephants and if you'll bird-sit tomorrow, I suppose I could keep this matter just between us."

Simba turned to the leader of the elephant herd. "I'm sorry," he said. "I won't let it happen again." To Nala, he whispered, "And bird-sitting will be a cinch!"

The next morning, Zazu met Simba and Nala near Pride Rock.

"This is Zinga," said Zazu.

A blur of colours zoomed past Simba and Nala. "That *was* Zinga," said Zazu. "Better catch up with her!"

"But Zazu—" Simba began.

"Just don't leave the Pride Lands," Zazu called as he flew off. "And meet me here at midday. Zinga's mother will be back then."

Nala looked around for Zinga. "Where'd she go?" she asked.

"I don't know, but we'd better find her," said Simba.

A burst of colour and feathers flew out of Rafiki's tree. "Off with you, young one," said Rafiki, laughing.

"There she goes!" Simba yelled. "Zinga!"

Zinga made a sudden sharp turn and flew straight towards Simba and Nala. She landed on Nala's back, then walked up to her head and perched there. "You must be the bird-sitters. Well, I already told Uncle Zazu I don't need bird-sitters. Thanks!" Zinga took off again.

"Where are you going?" Simba ran after her.

"Just out to play!" Zinga called.

"Oh." Simba said. He stopped running. "I suppose that doesn't sound too bad."

"Uh, Simba," said Nala, "isn't that what we usually say?"

Simba thought about it. They'd just been playing when they started the elephant stampede. "OH," he called, starting to run again. "Zinga, wait!"

Zinga didn't wait. She flew into a herd of zebras, dodging in and out of their stripes.

Simba got dizzy trying to keep track of her. Then Zinga upset some mother birds who were giving their babies flying lessons.

"Can't catch me!" Zinga called.

Simba and Nala were too out of breath even to try to catch her.

"That's it!" Simba flopped down in the shade of Rafiki's tree. "She can go and chase herself!"

Above them, Simba and Nala heard a laugh.

Rafiki peered down at them. "Zinga enjoys this game you play. Stop chasing her, and the game will change."

"What do you mean?" Nala asked.

Rafiki just hummed and turned away.

"I know," said Simba. "If we stop chasing Zinga, she'll come looking for us. All we have to do is wait where Zazu told us!"

"All right!" Nala sprinted away with Simba.

Neither of them saw Zinga flying towards the elephant's watering hole.

Simba lay back, his paws in the air. "Hey, this bird-sitting is easy. Nothing to—"

The ground began to shake. Simba and Nala stood up. The herd of elephants was stampeding towards them, with Zinga in the lead. "Run for your life!" Zinga yelled.

Simba and Nala leaped up onto some high rocks. Zinga landed near them, panting. The elephants ran past and around the rocks, their big feet crushing a

path into the ground. As the herd moved away, Simba and Nala frowned at Zinga.

"I didn't mean to," she said. "I was just playing with them, you know—pulling tails." She smiled weakly. "I didn't mean to make them stampede."

Simba pointed toward the last of the herd. "That, Zinga, is why we wanted you to stay close to us." Simba hoped he sounded like his father. "When you wander off, you get into trouble."

"That's right," added Nala. Out of the side of her mouth, she added, "You sound like Zazu."

Simba stared at her. Like Zazu?

"That is music to my ears, Nala!" Zazu said as he landed on the rocks.

"Oh, my, yes," said Zinga's mother as she joined them. "I can see why you picked these two for bird-sitting. I'm sure they don't give you any trouble."

Zazu smiled. "I'm sure they won't be giving me any trouble for a while."

Nala and Simba looked at each other and nodded. They were too tired to cause trouble—for a while.

A Closer Look

Feeding Time at the Zoo

What does a lion want for lunch? What snack might tempt a picky panda? Imagine preparing meals for thousands of different animals. They all have different needs. And not one can tell you what it wants!

That's the job that zoos face every day. Luckily, zoos have experts to help work out what the animals need in their diets.

Zookeepers will go to any length—or height—to feed the animals in their care!

A baby hippo gets a bottle, just like a human baby! But most of the food served at the zoo is prepared in a special kitchen.

They start by looking at what the animal eats in the wild. Then they come up with a diet that has the same nutrients. Nutrients are all the things in food that the animal needs to stay healthy.

Now it's up to the zoo chefs and zookeepers. They make sure that each animal gets the foods it needs. Mice, mealworms, meat mix—they're all on the menu at the zoo!

Animals in zoos don't usually get the same foods they would in the wild. Plants a giraffe would eat in Africa don't grow in Britain, for example.

A zoo panda shakes biscuits from a ball. Toys like this keep zoo animals from getting bored.

Instead, zoos use prepared foods. A monkey might get "Monkey Chow." An anteater might get "Instant Ant." These foods have all the necessary vitamins and minerals.

Zoos also feed little extras that the animals really enjoy. For example, monkeys get fruit and other treats as well as chow.

Please Don't Feed the Animals

If you've been to a zoo, you have seen signs telling you not to give food to the animals. Here's why:

Hundreds of people visit the zoo every day. If they all toss food to the animals, the animals will fill up on "junk" food. Just like people who snack too much, they won't be hungry at meal times. Then they won't get the nutrients they need to stay healthy!

Grazing animals munch on foods called "browse"—plant stems and leaves. Zoos go through a lot of browse. A single elephant eats 45 kilos of hay a day, along with 14 kilos of fruits and vegetables!

Sometimes animals get special goodies. In hot weather, zoo bears may chill out with bear "popsicles." These treats are oranges frozen in a bucket of water. The bears lick and play with the pops until they can pry the oranges out of the melting ice.

Zoo experts keep a careful watch on what the animals eat. The meals they are fed should keep the animals happy and healthy. Then the zoo chefs and zookeepers know they have done a good job!

Weighing In

Not too fat . . . not too thin. This baby bird is just the right weight! Zoo animals get regular checkups to make sure they are eating the correct foods.

A mushroom makes an excellent umbrella for a little frog!

Amazing Mushrooms

This is a great place for a fairy to rest!

There's something amazing about mushrooms. They spring up overnight. And they look magical—like little umbrellas, or seats for fairies.

What are mushrooms? They aren't plants. Plants make their own food, but mushrooms do not. They aren't animals. Animals move around, but mushrooms cannot. Mushrooms belong to a different family of living things. They are fungi.

Mushrooms grow almost everywhere. Look for mushrooms in damp soil and rotting wood. You'll be surprised at what you find!

Some mushrooms are so small, you can barely see them. But some grow bigger than footballs! Many mushrooms are shaped like little umbrellas. Others look like cups, balls, or shelves. They may be white, brown, red, yellow, or some other colour. Some mushrooms are lacy, and some even have spots!

There are hundreds of different kinds of mushroom. Top to bottom: White-capped mushrooms are common. The lacy mushroom looks pretty but smells rotten. Golden spoon-shaped mushrooms grow in parts of the United States. Pink umbrella mushrooms grow in Central America.

Did You Know?

Some mushrooms glow in the dark! These mushrooms make special chemicals that cause them to shine.

Many mushrooms are food for animals and people. But some mushrooms are poisonous. Only a mushroom expert can tell the difference between a safe mushroom and a deadly mushroom. That's why you should never ever eat a mushroom that you find growing wild!

Beware: These red mushrooms look pretty. But they are poisonous!

Don't pick the mushrooms, boys!

Long ago, people thought that toads made mushrooms poisonous by sitting on them. That's not true. But some people still call poisonous mushrooms "toadstools." And for these toads, mushrooms really *are* stools!

Shelves! Just the place for my fairy dust.

These bracket mushrooms look like shelves. They are growing from the side of a tree.

There's more to a mushroom than you can see. Hidden in the mushroom are tiny spores. They look like specks of dust. The spores drop from the mushroom. Wind and rain carry them away. If a spore lands on damp soil or a rotting log, it begins to grow. Soon new mushrooms push up through the soil.

And under the soil or inside the rotting log is a tangle of tiny white threads. These threads soak up the water and food that the mushroom needs to live!

Make Spore Prints!

1. Find a mushroom that has slits on the underside of the cap.
2. Remove the stem.
3. Put the cap, slits down, on a sheet of white paper. Cover it with a bowl and leave it overnight.
4. Lift the bowl and the mushroom. Spores will have fallen out, leaving a pattern on the paper. Now you have fungus fingerprints. And each one is different!

Doggone It, Stitch!

Stitch was waiting for Lilo to come home from school when Lilo burst into the house, carrying a puppy.

"Hi, Stitch!" Lilo called. "My neighbour Leilani asked me to look after her puppy, Rover, while she stays with her grandmother."

"Stitch wants to listen to Elvis," Stitch said.

"Not now," Lilo answered. "I have to look after Rover."

Stitch watched Lilo feed Rover and make him a bed. He watched her scratch Rover's ears and rub his tummy. She wasn't paying any attention to Stitch.

"Can we listen to Elvis now?" Stitch asked.

"I want to teach Rover tricks," Lilo said.

Stitch watched Lilo teach Rover to sit up and lie down. She showed him how to roll over. She threw balls for the puppy and gave him treats.

That evening, Nani and Lilo watched Rover play tug-of-war with the kitchen rug. "Oh, isn't he sweet!" Nani exclaimed. They laughed at everything Rover did. They weren't paying any attention to Stitch.

Stitch went to bed feeling a little sad and left out. Maybe if I behave like a puppy, he thought, Lilo will pay attention to me.

The next morning, Stitch tried to behave like Rover. He hid Lilo's shoes and chewed the kitchen rug. But that only made Lilo angry.

"Go to our room and stay there while I take Rover for a walk," she said to Stitch.

Stitch waited until Lilo and Rover had gone. Then he hurried outside and ran towards town.

Lilo and Rover came home in time for her to go to her hula class. Lilo couldn't find Stitch anywhere. She wondered why he wasn't at home. Stitch loved dancing the hula.

I'll just have to go without him, Lilo thought.

Stitch wasn't at home when she returned, either. "Have you seen Stitch?" she asked Nani and her friend, David.

Before they could answer, Cobra Bubbles the social worker knocked at the door.

"You need to hide Stitch," he told them. "Two scientists from the Centre for the Study of Aliens are looking for him. They want to take him to their laboratory and study him."

"But I don't know where Stitch is!" Lilo exclaimed. "He's vanished!"

“Well, I suggest you find him before the scientists do,” Cobra replied.

Lilo and Nani hurried to town to look for Stitch. Cobra Bubbles and David drove to the beach to look for him.

“Stitch has been acting strangely all day,” Lilo told Nani as they searched. “He’s been really naughty. He hid my shoes and chewed the rug. He behaved just like Rover!”

Suddenly, Lilo worked out where Stitch had gone. "Come on!" she shouted, grabbing Nani's hand. "I bet Stitch thought I liked Rover better because he was a sweet puppy. I bet Stitch went to the animal shelter to watch the puppies!"

Sure enough, when they reached the shelter, Stitch was there.

"Stitch learning to be cute like puppy," Stitch explained when he saw Lilo. "So Lilo like him again."

"Stitch, I like you just the way you are," Lilo answered. "Now, let's go home!"

But when they started to leave, they saw the two scientists coming towards them.

"Nani!" Lilo said. "We must do something!"

Nani spotted two mops in the shelter cupboard. She tied the mops onto Stitch so he looked just like a floppy puppy.

Lilo put a collar and lead on Stitch, and they walked slowly out of the shelter and past the scientists. The scientists watched Stitch suspiciously.

But just then, Cobra Bubbles and David drove up.

"Hey, scientists!" David yelled. "We've just seen an alien heading out to sea. You'd better hurry if you want to catch him. Hop in the car, and we'll take you there." The scientists jumped into the car, and Cobra Bubbles and David sped off.

Nani, Lilo, and Stitch were safe!

As soon as they got home, Lilo and Nani made a cake with pink icing and the word *'ohana* written on top.

As they were starting to eat the cake, Cobra Bubbles and David came in. "The scientists are heading out to sea to look for Stitch," Cobra said. "So he's safe for now."

"And look what I found at the beach," David said. He lifted a kitten out of a bag and put it on the floor.

"I thought she needed a good home," he said.

"How sweet!" Lilo said. Stitch watched everyone play with the kitten. But before he could start to feel left out again, the kitten climbed onto his lap and fell asleep. Stitch felt warm and happy inside.

"Stitch never had pet before," Stitch said. "Can Stitch keep kitten?"

"Yes," Nani answered. "In fact, I think that kitten has just adopted you as its family."

"And you know what that means," Lilo said.

Stitch nodded solemnly. "*'Ohana.* It means 'family.' And in a family, nobody—Stitch or kitten—gets left out!"

Treasure Boxes

It's fun to collect seashells. It's even more fun to use them to create pretty boxes. You can fill the boxes with precious treasures.

What You Need

What You Do

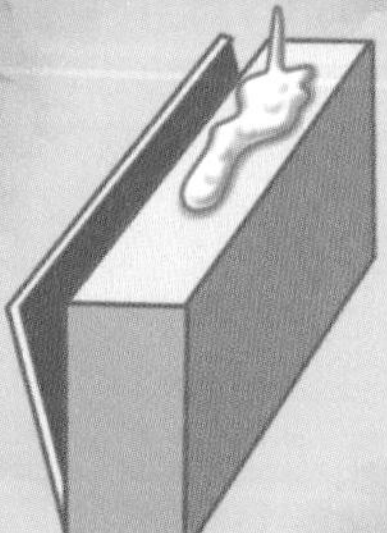

1. Spread glue on the four sides of the box. Use a paintbrush to smooth the glue out.

2. Sprinkle the coloured sand onto the gluey areas. Do this over a newspaper to catch any sand that doesn't stick. Make sure the sand completely covers the glue.

3. Spread the glue onto the top of the box. Smooth out the glue, but keep it quite thick.

4. While the glue is still wet, press the seashells into the glue. Make a nice decoration.

5. Let the box dry thoroughly. Then paint the shells with a coat of varnish, to give them a shiny finish.

6. Now fill your little treasure chest!

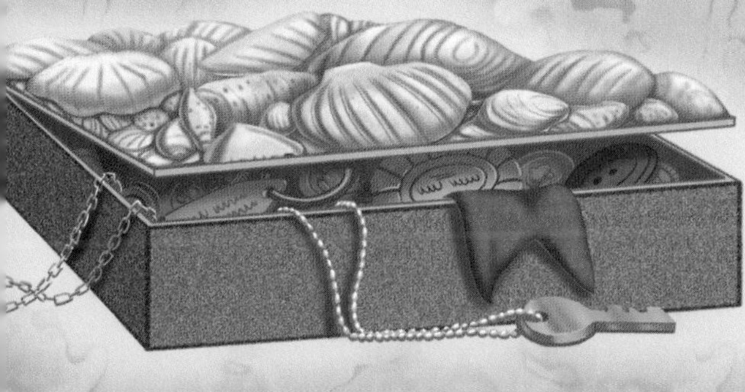

Stitch in Time

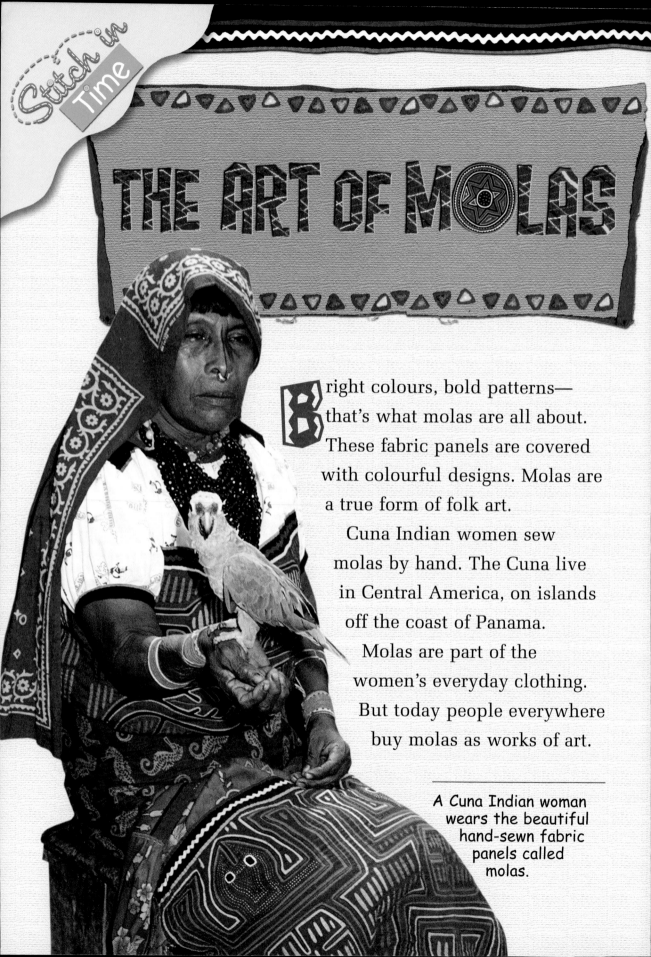

THE ART OF MOLAS

Bright colours, bold patterns—that's what molas are all about. These fabric panels are covered with colourful designs. Molas are a true form of folk art.

Cuna Indian women sew molas by hand. The Cuna live in Central America, on islands off the coast of Panama.

Molas are part of the women's everyday clothing. But today people everywhere buy molas as works of art.

A Cuna Indian woman wears the beautiful hand-sewn fabric panels called molas.

Each mola is made from many layers of different-coloured cloth. First, the mola maker draws a design on the top layer of cloth.

Then the layers of cloth are carefully cut and stitched. Details are added with coloured threads.It takes weeks to make each panel. A mola is like a sculpture in cloth.

Plants and animals—even imaginary ones—are often shown on molas.

This mola shows a farmer surrounded by animals. Can you spot them all?

A mola with birds . . . delightful!

Colourful parrots and a tropical fish mingle on this mola.

MOLA MAKING

Molas are made from many layers of different-coloured fabrics. The maker first draws the design on the top layer. Then she carefully cuts away layers to show the colours below.

A mola could show anything—even me!

Molas can have all sorts of designs. Some molas show the plants and animals of the Cuna homeland. The rain forests and oceans of this area are a natural wonderland. And the Cuna people love their wildlife.

. . . or me!

An owl swoops over a surprised woman's shoulder in this mola.

He looks a bit like my Dad!

Some molas show people fishing or farming. Others show scenes from history. Some show dreams. Some show folktales. And some just show circles, squares, and other shapes.

Today the Cuna also use lots of modern designs in their molas. Many of these molas are made to sell to tourists. But the most beautiful molas are the ones that the Cuna women make for themselves.

The women cover every inch of these special molas with designs. Making and wearing molas is a way for them to honour their community and their traditions.

MODER

Today, Cuna women include anything and everything in their mola designs. Magazine ads and pictures from books become subjects for many designs. Cartoon characters are also popular. Some molas even show things that the Cuna have never seen. How about snowmen and Santa Claus? Teenage Mutant Ninja Turtles? Why not!

Birdie, Be Mine!

These birds are in love. They're lovebirds!

Who is *your* Prince Charming?

Spring is the time when birds pair up to raise their families. And male birds go all out to attract females. They dance. They show off their feathers. And they do all sorts of tricks. Male birds will do almost anything to get a mate!

Show Off! A peacock wows a female with his beautiful feathers!

Puff Up! A male frigatebird has a red throat pouch. When a female comes near, he puffs up his pouch. She can't resist him!

Dance! A blue-footed booby dances for his mate. He hops around, flaps his wings, and whistles. It's quite a show!

Give Gifts! A male great blue heron brings his mate a stick. It's his way of showing that he can help build a good nest!

Just a Touch of Magic

King Horace and Queen Clarabelle loved to dance, and they often gave fabulous royal balls. Their daughter, Princess Daisy, however, had no interest at all in parties. True to her name, she loved flowers and plants and everything neat and pretty. She kept the royal landscapers and decorators quite busy.

One day the queen had an idea. "Daisy, dear, let's have a Beautiful Cottage Contest. You can be the judge!" she suggested.

"What fun!" Daisy exclaimed. "What will the most beautiful cottage winner win?"

The king said, "No matter how humble he is, the winner will be invited to the next ball!"

The whole kingdom was buzzing with the news. Everyone entered the Beautiful Cottage Contest—except a poor fisherman named Donald Duck.

Donald wanted to go to the ball and dance with the princess more than anything, but he knew his humble, tumble-down cottage could never win. Those messy chipmunks Chip 'n' Dale just wouldn't stay away.

Donald didn't have much luck fishing, either. He kept seeing himself dancing with the princess. He shook himself out of his daydream. "What's that?" he said, pulling in his fishing line. An odd-looking stick was tangled in the line.

"Maybe it's a magic wand! And I can use it to win the contest and go to the ball!" He quickly rowed home.

Donald looked at the wand. “No magic words on it. I wonder how it works.” He pointed it at the leaky roof and cried, “Patch the thatch!”

The roof didn’t patch itself, but a huge pile of new thatch appeared. Donald spent the rest of the day re-thatching his roof.

As he crawled into bed that night, Donald tossed the wand on the table, where it landed on top of his can of blue paint. “Maybe I’ll paint all the windowsills tomorrow,” he muttered. “Wish I had enough paint for the shutters and door, too.”

The next morning, Donald took the paintbrush and can of blue paint from the table and tripped. “Waak!” he cried, tumbling over five more cans of blue paint. “Hey! There’s enough blue paint for all the woodwork! My magic wand is still working!”

By the end of the afternoon, his roof, windowsills, shutters, and door definitely looked a lot brighter. Unfortunately, the dull grey walls just looked duller and greyer.

"What I need is whitewash!" Donald cried. Trying magic again, he used the wand—and a large tub of whitewash appeared. Then he found an old broom for a brush. Donald sighed and set to work. "Wish I had a couple more hands and brooms for this job."

After a few minutes, he heard a familiar chattering. "Not again!" he said when he saw Chip 'n' Dale. Each was holding a pint-sized broom dripping with whitewash. Donald smiled. Instead of causing trouble, the two chipmunks were gleefully dabbing whitewash on the cottage walls.

When Donald and the chipmunks had finally covered every dingy spot with whitewash, all three of them were as white as the cottage walls.

Donald ran to the lake and washed off. Sputtering and dripping, he looked up at his cottage. The new thatch, the blue woodwork, and the whitewashed walls looked even better—except for the

speckles of whitewash on the bushes. Donald ran inside and tossed the wand onto the table. It landed on a pair of pruning shears.

After Donald changed into dry clothes, he noticed a sparkle on the pruning shears. As he picked them up, the wand rolled off the table and landed on Donald's wet clothes.

Outside, Donald started snipping. Snip, snip here. Snip, snip there. It was almost as if the shears were snipping on their own.

Suddenly the snipping stopped. "Waak!" Donald cried. "That bush looks like me! And that one looks

like Princess Daisy!" Donald would have fainted there and then, but he heard trumpets blaring. Princess Daisy was coming!

Donald raced inside to look for some clean clothes. Much to his surprise, he found some under the wand. But then he saw the dirty dishes, clothes, and dust everywhere, along with Chip 'n' Dale's dirty paw prints. "I just wish the inside was as pretty as the outside," he said with a sigh. Tossing the wand on the floor, he went outside to greet the princess.

Donald bowed as Princess Daisy descended from the royal carriage. “What a sweet cottage,” she said.

“Thank you, Your Princess-ness.” Donald took off his hat and bowed.

“New thatch,” the princess quietly said. “Fresh whitewashing. Woodwork painted my favourite shade of blue!” Then Princess Daisy saw the bushes. “Oh!” she cried. “Is that. . .? And that. . .? Why, how delightful!” Donald blushed. “Donald, you have almost won the Beautiful Cottage Contest! All I need is a peek inside your sweet, humble cottage.”

"Oh, no, Your Princess-ness, you don't really want to see the inside of my cottage. Not sweet. Too humble. Too . . . late."

Princess Daisy had opened the door. "What?" cried Donald.

"Delightful!" she said. "I love it! The furniture—Chippendale, isn't it?"

Neither of them heard a fairy's voice outside. "So that's where you are, you naughty wand! Come on . . ." The wand floated out of the window.

The next time Donald heard trumpets blaring, they were for him! He arrived at the ball in a brand new suit of clothes. And Donald Duck, a humble fisherman, danced at the ball with Princess Daisy all night long.

Let's meet

Sister Act

Serena and Venus: sisters, tennis stars, best friends.

No one can hit a tennis ball like Venus Williams. Well, no one but her sister Serena!

Venus and Serena Williams are top stars in women's tennis. And these winning sisters are best friends, too.

Venus and Serena have been playing tennis since they were four years old. Playing singly, each sister has won major tennis titles. And when they play together, the Williams sisters are hard to beat!

Serena has a lot of power. She can return a tennis ball at great speed.

Winners on the Court

There are four top events in tennis. They are the Australian Open, the French Open, England's Wimbledon, and the U.S. Open. Venus has won the singles titles at Wimbledon and the U.S. Open. And Serena has won all four!

The sisters are strong athletes. Venus, 23, is more than 6 feet tall. She can hit a tennis ball at 200 km per hour!

Serena is about a year younger than Venus. She's a little shorter, too. But she's much stronger. She blasts the ball with a powerful two-handed backhand.

How's this for a prize? Venus holds the women's singles trophy at Wimbledon.

Growing Up

Sisters and pals: On the tennis court as kids (top). With beaded braids and braces as teenagers (middle). At a fashion awards show in their twenties (bottom).

Venus and Serena are rivals on the tennis court. But off the court they are very close. They practice together and enjoy many of the same activities.

The girls grew up in California and Florida. They have three older sisters. Venus and Serena started playing tennis as kids.

The sisters say their close family life has helped them succeed in professional tennis. Their parents usually travel with them, and their dad has been their coach.

But they know there's more to life than tennis. Venus and Serena are both interested in careers in fashion design. Serena is also thinking about an acting career.

Venus and Serena are double trouble on the tennis court. That must be why they were asked to do ads for this chewing gum!

When the Williams sisters were growing up, Venus helped her younger sister Serena learn to play tennis. But now Serena is more than a match for her big sister. And when Venus and Serena face each other in a tennis game, Serena usually wins.

Fans pack the stands when the Williams sisters are on the court. People love to watch these amazing sisters in action!

The Williams sisters are so famous, there are even Venus and Serena dolls!

Creature Feature

Perfect Partners

Uh-oh! This playground is only for sea anemones—not flounders!

Clownfish and sea anemones have a special relationship. Each gets something from the other.

Fishy Friends

A sea anemone looks like a flower, but it's really an animal. The anemone has lots of arms that look just like petals. But if a fish runs into those arms, they sting!

However, there is one fish—the clownfish—that can live right among the anemone's arms! This fish gobbles up tiny bits of ocean food that's trapped there. The fish gets a meal. The anemone gets cleaned. They are partners.

CLEANER CHUMS

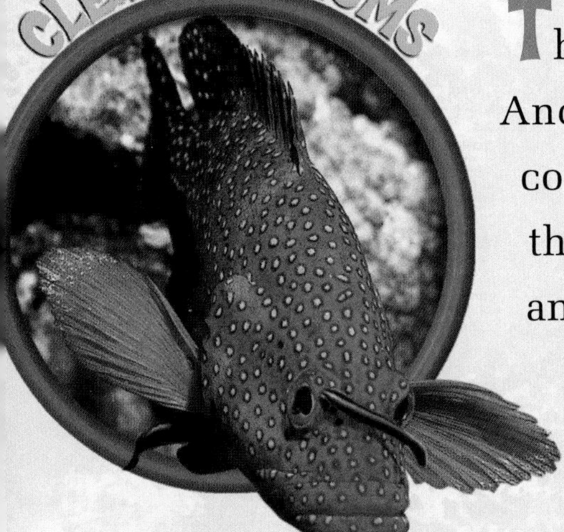

There are many more animal partners. And some of them make very odd couples! But working together helps them survive. For example, like sea anemones, lots of fish can't groom themselves. They count on other animals to help. And like the clownfish, the groomers get a meal.

Little groomers like the cleaner wrasse (above) and the cleaner shrimp (below) aren't afraid of their big partners!

FEATHERED FRIENDS

Birds called egrets like to stay close to big animals like this African rhinoceros. They are looking for a meal! As the rhino stomps through the grass, it startles insects. The insects fly up to get out of the way. And the egrets eat the insects. The rhino gets something out of the partnership, too. If the egrets see danger, they warn the rhino. They call out, flap their wings, and even hop onto the big animal's back.

Oxpeckers are tiny African birds that help out in a very big way. They eat ticks that they pluck from the fur of large animals. Besides keeping the animals free of pests, they also warn of danger. An oxpecker will even sit on its big pal's head and peck, peck, peck to make its point!

An oxpecker spends most of its life riding around on a big animal such as an antelope (above) or a buffalo (below). The bird even sleeps on its animal!

RIDE 'N' HIDE

Sponges are simple ocean animals. They eat bits of food that float past in the water. And they stay in one spot—unless a sponge crab comes along.

The sponge crab sticks a piece of the sponge on its shell. The sponge grows, hiding the crab from its enemies. And riding around on its crab, the sponge gets a steady stream of food bits.

Here's an odd pair—a sponge and a crab. I wish *I* had a sponge to protect me!

SWEET DEALS

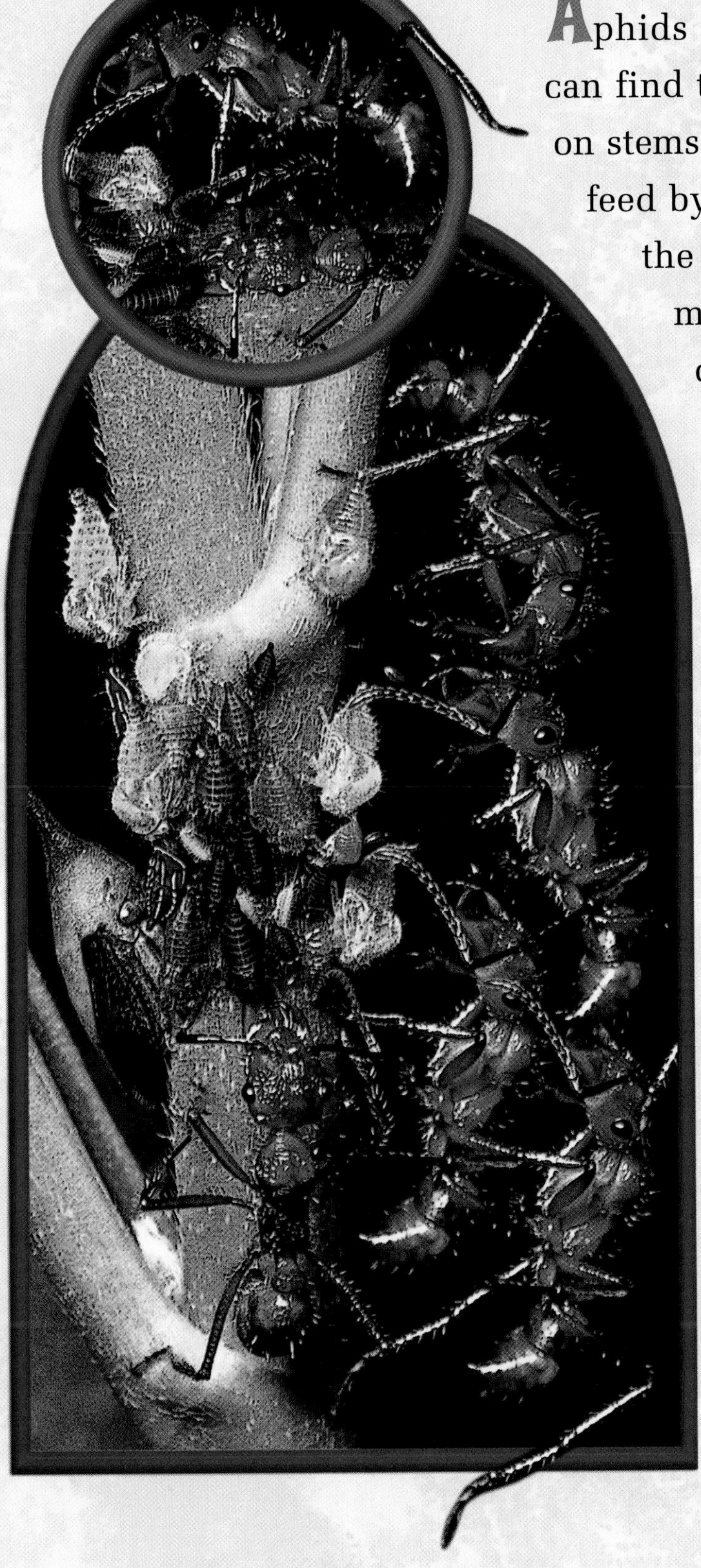

Aphids are tiny insects. You can find them on garden plants, on stems and under leaves. They feed by sucking juice from the plants. And they make a sweet substance called honeydew.

Ants love honeydew. To get it, some ants look after aphids the way people look after bees! The ants protect the little insects and move them to good feeding spots. In exchange, the ants collect the honeydew from the aphids. Like other animal partnerships, it's a sweet deal for both!

The Last Laugh!

What does a hippo have if its head is hot and it sees spots?

A polka-dotted sock over its head!

What did the sunken ship say when it was surrounded by sharks?

Help! I'm a nervous wreck!

What did the beaver say when it heard a chain saw?

They're playing my song!

Why do mother kangaroos hate rainy days?

Because their children have to play inside!

Why didn't the skeleton go to the ball?

It had no body to go with!

What's a sheep's favourite fruit?

Baaa-nanas!

What did the Cinderella fish wear to the ball?

Glass flippers!